I AM NOT FROM HERE

A book for anyone who's ever felt out of place in this world

Written by
Atlas

CONTENTS

One..4
THE OUTCAST 4

Two 8
A House Is Not a Home...8

Three.. 12
The Search for Love..12

Four.. 16
Alone in a Crowd..16

Five 20
Unspoken Pain...20

Six.. 24
The Bedside Conversations...24

Seven.. 28
Attempts and Angels...28

Eight 32
Overflow..32

Nine.. 36
God Knows My Name...36

Ten 40
Maybe This Is the Book..40

Eleven.. 42
Afraid to love, or be loved..42

Twelve	***46***
Tired but Trying	46
Thirteen	***50***
I Feel Everything	50
Fourteen	***54***
The Mirror	54
Fifteen	***58***
The Bridge	58
Sixteen	***62***
The Quiet Goodbye	62
Seventeen	***66***
Soft Doesn't Mean Weak	66
Eighteen	***70***
Let Love Find Me	70
Nineteen	***74***
Fading Echoes	74
Twenty	***78***
What I Want to Tell the Younger Me	78
Twenty One	***82***
If This Is the Last Page	82
Final Prayer	***86***
P.S.	***87***

One
THE OUTCAST

I've always felt like an outcast in this world.
Like I was placed here by mistake — a soul dropped in the wrong timeline, in the wrong place, among people who would never really understand me.

Growing up, I was surrounded by people — family, friends, noise, life — but inside, it was always quiet. Empty.
I had a mom, a dad, a sister — and anyone from the outside would look and think, what more could I ask for?

But there was always more to the story than anyone could see.
Because while I was surrounded, I never truly felt seen.

I had to grow up fast.
Way too fast.
Before I even knew how to spell "childhood," I was already fighting battles most people don't face in a lifetime.

I learned to protect myself.
To carry my own pain like armor.
To cry without a sound, and to smile like I wasn't breaking.

And when you grow up like that, it shapes you. It builds walls around you that even you can't see over.
Sometimes I wonder if this world was ever meant for someone like me.
People chase dreams, bags, cars, houses, attention.
But me?
I've learned how to live without.
I've learned how to breathe in a room full of people and still feel like the only one there.
And I've learned that love — real love — is not always found where it's supposed to be.

There's this loneliness that doesn't leave, even in laughter.
This ache that doesn't need a reason — it just… exists.
I could be standing in a room full of people who say they care about me and still feel like I'm floating in a different world.

I've always been the one who gives — my time, my care, my heart, even when it's tired.
I've made others feel seen, heard, and whole…
But when I come home at night, lie in bed, and face the silence — I realize no one really does the same for *me*.

I've been called an angel more times than I can count.
People say I bring peace, that I'm a light in their life.
But even angels get tired of flying.
Even light wants to rest in the warmth of someone else's love.
There were times I asked God, "Why did You put me here? Why give me this heart, this depth, this sensitivity — in a world that doesn't know what to do with it?"

And the answer never came in words — but in the quiet, I realized…
Maybe I wasn't meant to fit in.
Maybe I was meant to be a mirror — to show people the parts they forgot to love in themselves.
Maybe being an outcast wasn't a punishment.

Maybe it was protection.

Still… I long for home.
Not a place, but a feeling.
A space where my soul can exhale.
Where I don't have to explain myself.
Where I am loved not for what I do, or how much I give — but simply because I *am*.

Two

A HOUSE IS NOT A HOME

They say if you have a roof over your head, food on the table, and a family around you — you should be grateful. And I was. I *am*.

I had a mom. A dad. A sister.

On paper, it looked complete — the picture-perfect family. But what they don't tell you is that a house can be full of people... and still feel *empty*.

Because love isn't about presence. It's about connection.
And I never really felt it — not in the way my heart needed it.
There were moments I would be in the same room with them, but it felt like I was screaming into silence.
Like I was invisible, even when they were looking right at me.
I craved something I couldn't even name at the time.
Warmth. Reassurance. Safety. A gentle hand on my back telling me it's okay to cry.

Instead, I became my own caretaker. My own comfort. My own lifeline.

They say they loved me.
They just didn't know how to show it.
But what do you do with love that never arrives in a language you understand?

There were birthdays, dinners, occasional smiles.
But no real closeness.
No "How are you really?"
No hugs that felt like home.
Just distance — even while we lived under the same roof.

Sometimes I wonder if they even knew how much I was carrying.
The thoughts. The silence. The pain I never dared speak aloud.
And maybe they were carrying their own too — too broken themselves to give love away.
But when you're a child, you don't see that.
You just feel the absence.
The coldness in warm spaces.

And so I stopped expecting.
I stopped hoping.
I trained myself not to need.
Because needing only led to disappointment.

But deep inside, I still searched.
For a parent in someone else.
For home in other people's arms.
For the love I never received, tucked into strangers who looked at me with kind eyes.

And then…
I lost my father.

And with that, I realized — there's no going back.
No more hoping for the love I once wished he would give.
No more time to rewrite the story.
Just silence… and a memory that never hugged back.

I still carry respect.
I still carry prayers for them.
But I had to stop expecting from people who never learned how to pour love into me.
Because that expectation was slowly killing me.

A house is not a home.
A roof doesn't mean safety.
Walls don't always protect.

Home is where you're understood.
Where your soul can be soft.
Where you're not punished for feeling too much or needing too deeply.

And one day, maybe I'll build that home.
For myself.
Or for someone else who needs it.
The home I never had — but always dreamed of.

Three
THE SEARCH FOR LOVE

I've spent my life searching for something I never fully received.
Not money.
Not success.
Not validation.

Just love.
That *real* kind.
The one that doesn't fade when you're not perfect.
The one that doesn't make you beg for attention.
The one that sees you — and stays.

I don't think people realize what it does to someone when they grow up without feeling truly loved.
You spend the rest of your life trying to find it — in words, in looks, in people, in places, in moments that never last.

I gave so much of myself, hoping someone would finally give back.
And at first, they do.

They feel the warmth I offer. They say I'm different, rare, beautiful in a way the world has forgotten.
They call me light. They call me healing. They say I'm too good to be true.

But maybe that's the problem.

Sometimes, love scares people.
Not because it's wrong — but because it's real.

And real love demands something deeper.
It brings out people's vulnerability.
It forces them to look at the parts of themselves they're not ready to share.
So instead of diving in, they hesitate.

They test the waters.
They pull back just when it starts to matter.
They start believing it won't last.
That it's too good.
That if they fall, they'll lose something — so instead, they never truly *try*.
They keep one foot out the door, just in case.
And that half-love hurts more than being alone.

I've realized that not everyone is afraid of being unloved.
Some people are afraid of being *truly loved*.
Because love, in its purest form, asks for presence, commitment, and truth.
And not everyone is ready for that.

But I've always been ready.

I know I'm different.
And I don't say that from a place of ego or pride — but from experience.
I've seen the way I love.
The way I show up, stay consistent, give without keeping score.
I'm not the regular boy, or the regular girl, who sees love as a transaction.

As an escape.
As a shortcut to fill a void.

I don't fall in love because I'm lonely.
I fall because I believe in connection.
Because I still believe that love — real, rooted, lasting love — is possible.

Maybe I haven't found it yet.
But I've *become* it.
And even if people don't always know what to do with someone like me — someone who feels deeply, gives fully, and expects nothing but honesty in return —
I'd still rather be who I am, than settle for less than love.

Chapter Four
ALONE IN A CROWD

There's a kind of loneliness no one talks about.
It doesn't show up in silence or solitude.
It shows up in laughter.
In group photos.
In dinner tables filled with people who smile but don't see you.

It's being surrounded — but not connected.
Included — but not understood.
Visible — but not *felt*.

That's the kind of loneliness I've lived with.

I've walked into rooms where everyone seemed to be having the time of their lives,
and still felt like a stranger.
I've smiled in conversations while my heart was somewhere else —
quieter, darker, more honest.

And the truth is, I've mastered the art of pretending.
Of being "okay."
Of giving energy, jokes, presence —
while wondering if anyone notices that something inside me is missing.

Most people don't.

Because I've always been the strong one.
The giver.
The listener.
The one who makes others feel seen, safe, special.

But when the night ends…
I go home, close the door, and sit with a silence that hugs me tighter than any human has.

And I ask myself the same quiet question:
"Who checks on the one who checks on everyone else?"

Sometimes I want to scream.
Not for attention — but for connection.
For someone to really ask how I'm doing,
and wait for the truth.
Not the "I'm good."
Not the "Just tired."
But the real, unfiltered version of me that I keep locked behind tired eyes and practiced smiles.

People love the light in me.
But they don't stay long enough to witness the shadows.
They enjoy the version of me that uplifts them —
but rarely hold space for the version that breaks down at 2 a.m.
wondering why they always leave.

And so I learned to keep certain parts of me quiet.
Not because I'm afraid to feel,
but because I know most people aren't ready to hold what I carry.

It's not that I'm asking for too much.

I've never needed grand gestures or constant attention.
I don't want to be chased or worshipped.

Just… *understood*.
Just *met halfway*.

I don't demand love — I give it.
But even the strongest hearts need a place to rest.
This isn't a cry for help.
It's a confession —
that sometimes, the loneliest place to be is in the middle of people who don't truly know you.

And maybe one day, I'll be in a room —
not just seen, but *felt*.
Not just heard, but *understood*.
Not just surrounded — but *held*.

Until then, I keep walking.
Alone, but honest.

Five
UNSPOKEN PAIN

There's a kind of pain that doesn't make a sound.
It doesn't show in bruises or in broken bones.
It hides in the quiet moments.
In the long stares.
In the deep sighs when no one is watching.

That's the pain I've known.
People look at me and see someone strong.
Collected.
Kind.
Still standing.

But they don't see the parts of me that had to survive things I never asked for.
The trauma.
The betrayal.
The moments that broke something sacred inside me... before I even knew what sacred meant.

I've been abused.
Taken for granted.
Molested.
Neglected.
Lied to.
Forgotten.

And what's worse — I carried it all *in silence*.

Because who would believe me?
Who would understand?
Who could handle the truth of what I've seen, felt, endured?

So I swallowed it.
I learned to function with a broken heart and a frozen smile.
I became so good at hiding the cracks, I started to forget they were there.
Until they started bleeding in ways I couldn't control.

There were nights I wanted to scream.
But I knew no one would hear me the way I needed to be heard.
Not with sympathy.

But with presence.
With someone simply saying: *"I see you. I believe you. And I'm here."*

But that never came.

So I became my own witness.
My own healer.
My own quiet hero.

I rebuilt myself from the ground up — not because I wanted to, but because I had no choice.
No one was coming to save me.

And maybe that's what made me different.
Resilient.
Rooted.

But the truth is… even now, parts of that pain still live in me.
In the way I flinch at certain tones.
In the way I overthink simple things.
In the way I keep people close — but not too close.

Because when you've been hurt deeply, love becomes both a longing and a risk.

There's a scar on my spirit — not because I'm weak, but because I've lived.
Because I've walked through fire and didn't let it kill me.

I don't wear my pain like a badge.
But I also won't pretend it didn't happen.

It made me who I am —
Not bitter.
Not broken.
But awake.

And maybe I'll never tell the full story out loud.
Maybe some things are meant to stay between me and God.
But I will say this:

If you've ever carried a storm inside you, quietly, while smiling at the world —
You're not alone.

Some of us were born to feel deeper, hurt harder, and still rise anyway.

Six
THE BEDSIDE CONVERSATIONS

The world always goes quiet at night. No distractions.
No noise.
No masks left to wear.
Just me… and the thoughts I've been running from all day.

I lay there, staring at the ceiling, sometimes in complete darkness —
and that's when the real conversations begin.
Not with anyone else.
Just me, and the version of myself I don't always let people see.

It's in those late-night hours that the loneliness hits the hardest.
Not because I don't have people around me.
But because I realize how few of them actually know me.

I'm the one who checks in on others.
The one who makes sure everyone else feels seen, loved, important.
But when the lights go out and the door closes…

who checks on me?

That's the question I've asked myself more times than I care to admit.
And not in a bitter way. Not in self-pity.
But just... honesty.

There's something about a bed that becomes a confession booth.
It knows your tears.
It holds your weight — not just your body, but your burdens.
It hears your prayers.
And sometimes, it's the only witness to the version of you the world never sees.

Sometimes I talk to God.
Sometimes I just talk to the ceiling.
Sometimes I talk to no one — just the silence that seems to understand me more than most people do.

And I say things like:

"Why do I feel so much?"
"Why does love always seem to escape me?"
"What would it feel like to be held — not physically, but emotionally?"
"Am I really as strong as they say... or just numb?"

These aren't dramatic thoughts.
They're just truths that visit me when the world stops moving.

In the daylight, I wear grace well.
I smile. I function. I even shine.

But at night, I just want to be.
Without performing.
Without explaining.
Without proving anything.

I want someone to lay beside me, not for comfort — but for understanding.
Someone who doesn't need words to know what I'm feeling.
Someone who doesn't need to ask if I'm okay — because they already know when I'm not.

But most nights, it's just me.

And I've learned to be okay with that.
Not because I prefer it — but because I've had to.

These bedside conversations?
They keep me grounded.
They remind me of who I really am, beneath the surface.
They remind me that even if no one else hears me… I hear me.

And maybe that's where healing begins.

Seven
ATTEMPTS AND ANGELS

There were moments I didn't want to be here anymore. Moments when the pain felt louder than the hope. When I couldn't see a way forward, and the weight of it all made me wonder if checking out was the only option left.

I don't say that lightly.
But I also don't say it with shame.

Because when life hits you hard enough — when you feel invisible for long enough — you start asking yourself questions you never thought you would.

And I did.

I asked God to take me.
I wondered what it would feel like to finally rest.
To finally stop trying, giving, proving, surviving.
But something — or someone — always stopped me.

A thought.
A presence.
A whisper I couldn't explain.

Something telling me, *"Not yet."*

At the time, I didn't know what it was.
But looking back, I believe it was God.
Or maybe… an angel.
Maybe many.

There's no other way to explain the times I was so close to the edge, and still… didn't fall.
Didn't jump.
Didn't let go.

I'd feel a stillness in the middle of the storm.
A quiet tug in my spirit saying, "You're not done."
"There's more for you."

And maybe that "more" wasn't for me.
Maybe it was for the people I would one day help.
The strangers I'd meet.
The ones who would feel seen because I was brave enough to keep going.

I used to think angels had wings and halos.
But now, I know they come in many forms.
A kind word.
A song at the right moment.
A stranger's smile.
A deep breath that returns when you thought you lost it forever.

And maybe… even in my pain, I've become an angel for others, too.
Maybe that's what happens when you survive things you never speak of — you carry light without even realizing it.

I once prayed a simple prayer:
"God, if I have to suffer, at least let it mean something. Use me to help someone else cross their storm."

And somehow, that prayer became my path.

I still have days when I feel the darkness creep in.
But I no longer believe it has the final word.
Because every time I almost left… I stayed.
Not out of fear.
But out of faith.

And that faith, as small as it was, saved my life.

So if you're reading this… and you've ever stood at the edge —
know that angels are real.
And sometimes, the strongest thing you can do is stay.

Even when it hurts.
Especially when it hurts.

Because sometimes, the ones who almost leave…
are the ones who end up guiding others home.

Eight
OVERFLOW

There's something about the way I love that doesn't make sense to most people.
It's not calculated.
It's not cautious.

It's not given in pieces.
It *flows*.
Like a river that doesn't ask who's drinking — it just pours.
Quietly. Steadily. Unconditionally.

I don't love halfway.
I never have.

Whether it's a friend, a partner, a stranger — if I let you into my world, you'll feel it.
You'll feel the care.
The warmth.
The presence.
The realness.

And the truth is… it's not something I do.
It's something I am.

I am the overflow.

Because I know what it feels like to grow up empty.
To crave softness and not find it.
To be strong because you had no other choice.

So I became what I never received.

I became safe.
I became patient.
I became the one who remembers the small details.
Who checks in even when no one checks back.
Who gives not to impress — but to *heal*.

And yet… I've often found myself pouring into people who came with cracked hands.
No matter how much I gave, they couldn't hold it.
Not because they were bad — but because they weren't ready.

Sometimes people take my love for granted — assuming it will always be there, a bottomless well.
They don't always understand what it means to truly receive care.
They hesitate, question their own worthiness, or simply aren't able to meet it.

It's not that I love them any less when I pull back;
it's that I've learned to protect myself
from giving so much to someone who isn't sure about their own feelings.

Over time I realized:
people love the idea of being with someone like me—
they love the comfort of my care,
but they're not always in love with me.

I don't deserve to be a safety net for someone who isn't ready to love—
who's blinded by fear, held back by expectations, or simply unsure

how to express what they feel.

So I set boundaries.
Not because I stopped wanting to give,
but because I have to love myself enough to let go when their hands remain empty.

Because even a river needs its banks to keep flowing.
And I refuse to drown in the idea of love that was never meant for me.

Nine
GOD KNOWS MY NAME

There have been times when I felt invisible.
When I'd walk through life unnoticed, unheard, misunderstood —
as if the world had turned its face away and forgot I was here.

But somehow, even in the quietest moments…
I knew I was being watched.
Not by people.
But by something higher.
Something holy.

By God.

Because even when no one saw my tears, He did.
Even when my voice shook with prayers I didn't know how to finish, He heard them.
Even when I questioned everything — why I was here, why I felt so

much, why love kept slipping through my fingers —
He stayed.

Not with thunder.
Not with lightning.
But with whispers.
With presence.
With *grace*.

There's something sacred about knowing that even when the world misunderstands you,
God never does.

He knows my name.
Not the one the world gave me —
But the one He wrote on my soul before I ever took my first breath.

He knows the child in me who was never fully comforted.
He knows the protector I became.
He knows the giver, the dreamer, the fighter, the quiet storm.

He knows every version of me.
And still… He calls me *His*.

There were nights I almost gave up —
but I didn't, not because I was strong,
but because something in me believed.
Believed that He had a reason.
That this story I was living had meaning, even if I couldn't see it yet.
I've seen signs.

In people.
In moments.
In little coincidences that weren't coincidences at all.
In the way peace shows up when I least expect it.
In the way my heart settles when I whisper, *"Ya Allah, I don't know what You're doing, but I trust You."*

And when I sit in stillness…
I talk to Him.

Not with rehearsed prayers, but with the voice of a servant saying:

"God, I'm listening. I'm here.
I don't always understand, but I'm yours.
I am your servant.
I am here to worship you.
To serve you.
To live for you."

This world may never understand me.
But God does.
And that… that has to be enough.

Because He doesn't need me to be perfect.
He doesn't need me to pretend.
He just wants me present.
Sincere.
Alive.

I once thought my story was about pain.
Now I know — it's about purpose.
And every scar I carry is a verse in the chapter He has written for me.

So I keep going.
Not for the world.
But for Him.
For the one who knew me before I knew myself.
For the one who whispered, "Stay."
When I wanted to leave.

Because no matter what happens next —
I am known.
I am seen.
I am loved.
And God knows my name.

Ten
MAYBE THIS IS THE BOOK

I never thought I'd write this.
Not because I didn't have anything to say —
But because I had *too much*.
Too many feelings.

Too many wounds.
Too many chapters I didn't know how to tell without trembling.

But maybe… this is the book.

Maybe this isn't just a collection of words.
Maybe it's the home I've always needed.
A place to put everything I've carried in silence.
A place where my pain, my hope, my thoughts — finally have a voice.

Because for so long, I've been the one people turn to.
The strong one.
The understanding one.
The one who listens, who holds, who heals.

But I've rarely had the space to unravel myself.
To be held the way I hold others.
To be heard — not in passing, but with care.

So maybe this is that space.
These pages.
These moments.

I didn't start writing this to impress anyone.
I'm not here to prove anything.
I'm not chasing likes or applause.
I'm just… telling the truth.

My truth.

And maybe, just maybe, that truth will echo in someone else's heart.
Someone who's been carrying the same weight.
Someone who thought they were alone in their thoughts.
Someone who's been asking, *"Does anyone feel like me?"*
To that person — yes.
I do.
I've felt it.
I've lived it.
I'm still healing from it.

And maybe that's why I'm writing now.
Not because I've figured it all out,
but because I finally realized — I don't need to.

Sometimes the healing isn't in having the answers.
Sometimes, it's just in being honest.
In saying, "Here I am. These are my scars. *This is my heart."*

And if even one person reads this and feels seen —
then every silent night, every breakdown, every prayer,
was worth it.

So maybe this is the book.

Not the one I planned.
But the one I needed.
And maybe… the one you needed too.

Eleven
AFRAID TO LOVE, OR BE LOVED

I've always believed that love — the real kind — doesn't just happen.
It arrives.
When the time is right.

When the souls are ready.
When the heart has learned what it will never again settle for.

And so, I've waited.

Not out of fear.
Not because I'm picky.
Not because I'm holding out for some fantasy.

But because I know what I carry.
I know the kind of love I give.
I know that when I show up for someone, I don't come halfway.
I don't love in convenience.

I love in *depth*.

And that kind of love isn't meant for just anyone.

So I wait.
Not with bitterness, but with intention.
With a quiet hope that somewhere out there, there's someone who feels things the way I do.
Someone who's not afraid to meet me where I am — emotionally, spiritually, soulfully.

Someone who doesn't just want a relationship —
but a connection.

Not perfection.
Not performance.
Just presence.

I've had people come close.
People who saw the surface.
Who enjoyed the warmth of what I offer —
but didn't stay long enough to understand the depth behind it.

And I don't blame them.
Not everyone is meant to stay.
Some are meant to teach.
To awaken.
To remind you of what not to accept again.

But deep down...
there's still this quiet place in my heart that whispers,
"One day, someone will stay."

And not just stay — but see me.

See the softness I hide.
The strength I carry.
The cracks that tell my story.
The loyalty that runs through everything I do.
The light and the shadows — and love both.

Someone who doesn't run from the depth,
but dives into it with me.

I don't need perfect.
I don't need constant fireworks.
I just need something true.

Someone who listens.
Who remembers.
Who chooses me — every day — not because they have to… but because they want to.

And when that day comes — if it ever does — I'll be ready.

Not because I've been waiting in desperation.
But because I've been preparing in love.

Becoming whole.
Becoming honest.
Becoming the kind of person I've always hoped to find.

Because here's the thing…
I feel everything.

Call it intuition.
A sixth sense.
A knowing beyond words.
But I read energy before I read lips.
I see what people try to hide.
I hear the hesitation in their silence.
I notice every pause, every shift, every small gesture that others overlook.

I feel love — when it's pure.
But I also feel when it's hesitant.
When it's guarded.
When it's being rationed out piece by piece — afraid to be fully seen.

And I've had enough of that.

I don't want a love I have to guess.

Or chase.
Or decode.

I want someone who doesn't hold back —
Who doesn't love me in fractions.
Who doesn't hesitate to say, *"You're it. It's you. I'm here."*

Because when I love… I don't hold back.
And I deserve the same.
Someone who looks at me and says:
"I see all of you… and I'm not going anywhere."

Until then…
I'll keep waiting — not for perfection,
but for presence.

For someone whose love doesn't make me question what I already know:

That I am worthy.
That I am enough.
That I am meant to be loved — without holding back.

Twelve
TIRED BUT TRYING

Some days I wake up and I feel like I'm dragging the weight of a thousand invisible things.
And still — I get up.
I smile.

I show up.
I do what I need to do.
Not because I feel strong… but because I have to be.

The truth is…
I'm tired.
Not just physically.
But emotionally.
Spiritually.
Soul-tired.

Tired of pretending.
Tired of giving so much and receiving so little.

Tired of hoping.
Tired of holding myself together when all I want is to fall apart.

But I still try.

Not for the applause.
Not for the validation.
But because there's something inside me that refuses to give up.
Something that believes my story is not over yet.
That my life still has meaning — even on the days when it feels like I'm running on empty.

Trying doesn't always look heroic.
Sometimes, it's just showing up when you don't want to.
Sometimes, it's brushing your teeth when you feel numb.
Sometimes, it's answering a message. Or going for a walk. Or simply breathing.

And over the years, I've realized something else:

Material things don't move me anymore.
I stopped craving possessions at a young age.
I learned to be okay with not being okay.
And I found a contentment few ever reach.
I'm not desperate for status, for things, for more.
Nothing in this world shakes the peace I've found inside me.

Trying isn't loud.
But it's real.

And even though I'm tired…
even though some days feel like too much…
I'm still here.

Still showing up.
Still choosing to believe there's something ahead worth holding on for.

So if you're tired too —
know this:

You're not weak for feeling it.
You're human.
And if all you did today was keep trying —
and maybe let go of wanting more than you need —
I'm proud of you.

Because I know how heavy the unseen battles are.
And I know what it means to keep going anyway.

Thirteen
I FEEL EVERYTHING

I don't know how to explain it.
But I feel things…
before they're said.
Before they're shown.

Before they even fully arrive.
I can walk into a room and sense the energy like it's painted on the walls.
I can look at someone's eyes and know what their words are too afraid to say.
I can feel the distance someone is trying to hide, even when they smile.
Even when they pretend.

Call it intuition.
Call it a sixth sense.
Call it being "too sensitive."

But this is how I've always been.

And while some may see it as a burden —
for me, it's never been a choice.

I feel everything.

The joy that others can't contain.
The grief they try to bury.
The tension in a touch.
The hesitation in a hug.
The fear behind the silence.
The love in a glance that never makes it to words.

And when I say I love deeply — I don't mean just emotionally.
I mean energetically.
Soulfully.
I love with my presence, with my listening, with my ability to see someone fully — even when they think they're hiding.

But here's the truth…

It gets heavy.

Because when you feel everything —
you carry more than just your own emotions.
You carry the weight of unspoken things.
You pick up on heartbreaks that haven't been confessed.
You sense lies dressed as smiles.
You know when someone's holding back — and it stings, even if they think they're protecting you.

And the hardest part?
Most people don't realize you feel it.
Because you don't confront it.
You just know.
Quietly. Softly. Painfully.

I've had people love me with restraint, thinking I wouldn't notice.
But I did.
I always do.

And that's what makes this sensitivity both a gift... and a curse.

Because I know when I'm being loved fully — and when I'm not.
I know when someone is present in body, but not in soul.
And I can't pretend I don't feel the difference.

But still... I wouldn't trade this part of me.

Because it's also what allows me to connect.
To care in ways that others can't.
To comfort without needing words.
To love people in the places they haven't even healed yet.

So if I seem quiet sometimes — it's not because I don't care.
It's because I'm feeling too much at once.

And if I pull back — it's not rejection.
It's protection.
Because when you feel everything, you have to learn when to shield your soul.

But when I find someone who doesn't make me question their love...
who is present in every way — open, honest, unafraid —

I soften.
I expand.
I become everything I've always been —
without needing to hold anything back.

That kind of connection?
It's rare.
But I still believe in it.

Because I feel everything —
and I know when something's real.

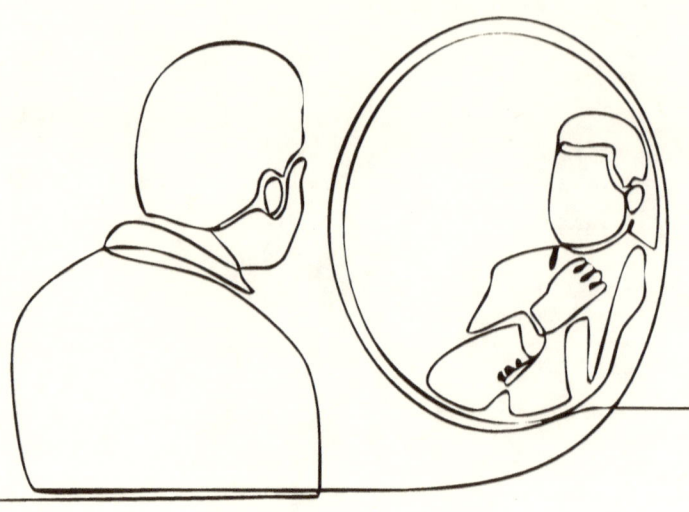

Fourteen

THE MIRROR

There's something sacred about looking at yourself.
Not just in passing.
Not to fix your hair.
But to really look.

To stand in front of the mirror and face the reflection that holds everything you've been through.

It's strange, how many times I've avoided my own eyes.
Not because I didn't recognize the face —
but because I *did*...
and I wasn't always proud of what I saw beneath it.

Behind the calm.
Behind the strength.
Behind the composure —
was someone quietly asking, *"Am I enough?"*

And some days, I didn't have an answer.

The mirror has seen me at my worst.
It has watched me cry in silence.
It has heard the words I was too afraid to say out loud.
It has held my shame.
My self-doubt.
My deepest ache.

But it has also witnessed my becoming.

The growth.
The healing.
The moments I chose to stand back up.
The days I decided to love myself again — even if just a little.

Because the truth is… the mirror doesn't lie.
It doesn't flatter or flatter back.
It reflects.

It shows you who you are —
but also who you're becoming.

And over time, I started to see something shift.

I started to see not just what hurt me,

but what healed me.
Not just what I lost,
but what I've built in the ruins.

Not just the brokenness —
but the quiet beauty of a soul that refused to stay shattered.

The mirror taught me that healing isn't glamorous.
It's messy.
It's raw.
It's crying one night and smiling the next.
It's forgiving yourself for not knowing better — and then learning anyway.

It's asking:
"Who am I without the pain?"

"Who am I if I stop proving my worth?"
"Who am I when I'm alone, and no one is watching?"

And slowly…
I began to answer.

I saw a person who's still learning.
Still hurting.
Still growing.
Still soft — even after everything.

A person who still hopes.
Who still loves.
Who still believes in goodness — even after being surrounded by darkness.

And that?
That's strength.

Real strength isn't loud.
It's not in how much you can carry —
It's in how deeply you can face yourself and still say:
"I am worthy. I am trying. I am healing. I am here."

Now, when I look in the mirror…
I no longer turn away.

I meet my eyes — not with shame —
but with grace.

Because I see someone who has survived more than anyone knows, and still dares to love, to believe, to be kind.

And if that's not beautiful —
I don't know what is.

Fifteen
THE BRIDGE

At some point in my life, I stopped asking,
"Who will help me?"
And started becoming the one who helped others.
Not because I had everything figured out.

Not because I was healed.
But because I knew what it felt like to be lost.
To be alone.
To be aching, and still pretending to be okay.

So I became the bridge.

The one people could walk across to find light.
To feel less alone.
To be reminded that they were seen, even when the world ignored them.

I have been the mother,
the father,

the brother,
the sister,
the lover,
the friend—
all the roles you needed me to fill,
because once upon a time, I had to fill every one of these roles for myself.

It wasn't something I set out to do.
It just… happened.

Maybe it was God answering my prayer.
That prayer I whispered so quietly one night,
"If I have to carry this pain, let it help someone else."

And maybe He did.

Because people began to find their way to me —
not just physically, but emotionally.
They opened up.
They cried.
They shared pieces of themselves they didn't show anyone else.
And somehow, I always knew how to hold them.

How to listen.
How to speak life into them.
How to remind them they mattered.

But being the bridge… it comes with weight.

Because while others are crossing,
you're still standing.
Still holding.
Still carrying your own brokenness while becoming a safe space for theirs.

And there are days I get tired.
Days I wish someone would ask how I'm doing.
Not out of obligation — but because they genuinely want to know.

But still… I don't regret it.

Because there's beauty in being a bridge.
In being the reason someone didn't give up.
In being the quiet voice that says,
"I know it hurts, but you're not alone."

Sometimes people call me an angel.
They say I have a light in me.
That I make them feel calm.
That I remind them of something sacred they'd forgotten in themselves.

And every time I hear it,
I smile.
Not because I believe I'm special —
but because I know what it took to become this version of me.

The darkness I crossed.
The silence I endured.
The nights I almost didn't make it.

And now...
I get to be the bridge for someone else.

So I keep standing.
I keep loving.
I keep giving — not because I have to... but because I get to.

Because maybe that's my purpose.
Not just to heal —
but to help others find the strength to begin healing too.

Sixteen
THE QUIET GOODBYE

Not every goodbye comes with a door slamming.
Not every ending is loud.
Some of the hardest goodbyes… happen in silence.
No arguments.

No final words.
Just distance.
Just a feeling.

Just that moment when you realize…
"They're no longer who they used to be."
Or worse,
"I'm no longer who I was when I loved them."

And so, you let go.
Quietly.
Softly.
Without applause.
Without closure.

Because you had to.

I've said goodbye to people who meant the world to me.
Not because I stopped caring — but because I had to start caring for myself more.

I've let go of connections that felt like home,
because they began to burn more than they warmed.
Because no matter how tightly I held on,
they were already halfway out the door.

Some people leave slowly.
With fewer messages.
Colder responses.
More space.

Others disappear all at once.
And you're left wondering if it was all in your head.

But the hardest goodbyes…
aren't to people.

They're to the versions of yourself that you had to shed in order to survive.

I've said goodbye to the me who begged for love.
The me who stayed silent to keep the peace.
The me who overextended just to feel wanted.

And I miss them sometimes.
Because they were soft.
They were hopeful.
They meant well.

But they didn't know how to protect themselves.

So I let them go.
Lovingly.
Gratefully.
Quietly.

Because not all evolution is loud.
Sometimes healing sounds like walking away.
Sometimes growth looks like deleting the message you wanted to send.
Sometimes peace means saying nothing at all.

And you learn that silence… is not always weakness.
Sometimes it's wisdom.
Sometimes it's your soul finally saying,
"It's time."

So I honor the goodbyes I never got to speak.
I forgive the ones who left without looking back.
And I forgive myself — for holding on too long, and for letting go too late.

Because every quiet goodbye…
taught me how to stay true to myself,
even when it hurt.

And in those moments —
I didn't just lose someone.
I found me.

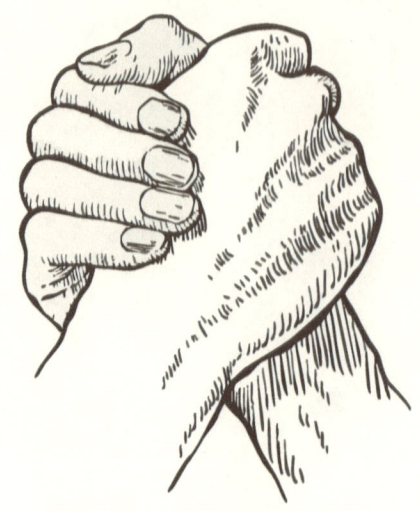

Seventeen
SOFT DOESN'T MEAN WEAK

For the longest time, I thought I had to toughen up.
To harden my heart.
To be colder, less emotional, less giving.
Because it felt like being soft made me a target — for misunderstanding, for mistreatment, for pain.

But I was wrong.

Softness is not weakness.
It never was.

In fact, the softest people I know are the ones who've been through the most.
Who've been broken, yet still choose to love.
Who've been let down, yet still show up.
Who carry storms in their chest and still offer others clear skies.

That's not weakness.
That's power.

And I've learned — slowly, and sometimes painfully — that I don't have to stop being gentle to survive this world.
I don't have to change the way I love just because others couldn't receive it properly.
I don't have to apologize for feeling deeply.
For being moved by small things.
For caring "too much."

That is *who I am*.
And I refuse to see it as a flaw.

Because being soft in a hard world is a rebellion.
It's courage.
It's resistance to becoming numb.

Yes, I feel things intensely.
Yes, I give people the benefit of the doubt.
Yes, I believe in kindness — even when it's not returned.
But that doesn't make me naïve.
That makes me human.

And if my softness makes someone uncomfortable —
that's not my burden to carry.

I'm not here to prove my worth by acting like I don't care.
I'm not here to shrink myself to fit into hardened spaces.

I've cried and still stood tall.
I've bent, but didn't break.
I've loved — even when I wasn't loved back — and that's a strength many don't understand.

Because anyone can be cold.
Anyone can shut down.
Anyone can run.

But it takes real courage to stay kind.
To open your heart — again and again — knowing it might get bruised.

I'm not weak.
I'm gentle — and grounded.
And I no longer see the two as opposites.
I've learned to own my tenderness.
To protect it.
To give it wisely.
And to wear it like armor, not like shame.

So if you're someone who feels deeply…
who loves with intention…
who moves through the world with empathy instead of ego —
don't let anyone make you feel small for that.

You don't need to become colder to be respected.
You don't need to be harsh to be heard.
You can be loving and still have boundaries.
You can be kind and still command strength.

This world doesn't need less softness.
It needs more *honest hearts*.
More calm in the chaos.
More people who dare to stay kind — even when it's hard.

So no — I'm not "too soft."
I'm just real.
And if that makes someone uncomfortable…
maybe they haven't met love in its purest form yet.

Eighteen
LET LOVE FIND ME

For most of my life, I was searching.
For love.
For belonging.
For someone who would hold me with the same care I gave so freely.

I tried.
I gave.
I waited.
I believed.

And sometimes… I begged in ways I didn't realize.
Not with words,
but with presence.
With over-understanding.
With silent hopes I kept folding into every smile.

But I'm not doing that anymore.

I'm done chasing love.
Done trying to prove that I'm worthy of being chosen.
Done trying to earn something that should arrive freely, naturally, honestly.

Because I know who I am now.
And I know what I carry.
And I don't need to be found by love if it's not ready to see me.

I don't want a love that arrives with hesitation.
Or one that only knows how to take.
I don't want to be someone's emotional rehab.
I don't want to be someone's halfway home.

I want a love that's ready.
Rooted.
Soft and steady.
The kind that doesn't make me question myself.
The kind that doesn't feel like work to receive.

Because love...
real love...
isn't just about touch, or time, or even emotional connection.

Love is when you want to see someone become the best version of themselves —
not for you, but for them.
It's when their peace matters more than your pride.
When their growth brings you joy.
When their healing feels like your own.

Love is a reassurance —
a safe place.
It's the kind of presence that says, *"You don't have to be perfect. I've got you anyway."*

It's patient.
It's nurturing.
It gives freedom, not fear.
Support, not silence.

Love says: *"I choose you — and I want you to become everything you're meant to be."*

And that's the only kind of love I'm open to now.
So now…
I let love find me.
Not because I've given up on it —
but because I finally trust that the kind of love I deserve can't be forced.
It shows up in divine timing.
It recognizes me because it reflects me.
It walks in and says,
"There you are. I've been looking for you too."

And when it does —
I'll know.

Because this time, I won't feel the need to overgive.
Or overexplain.
Or overstay in places where my soul doesn't feel safe.

This time, I'll be ready to receive.
To soften.
To trust that love can feel gentle, not urgent.
Whole, not heavy.
Sacred, not desperate.

Until then, I'll be here.
Living.
Becoming.
Loving myself in ways I once begged others to.
And creating space —
not for anyone…
but for the right one.

Because the kind of love I need doesn't arrive through searching.
It arrives through *alignment*.

And when it's time…
love will find me.

Whole.
Present.
And already at peace.

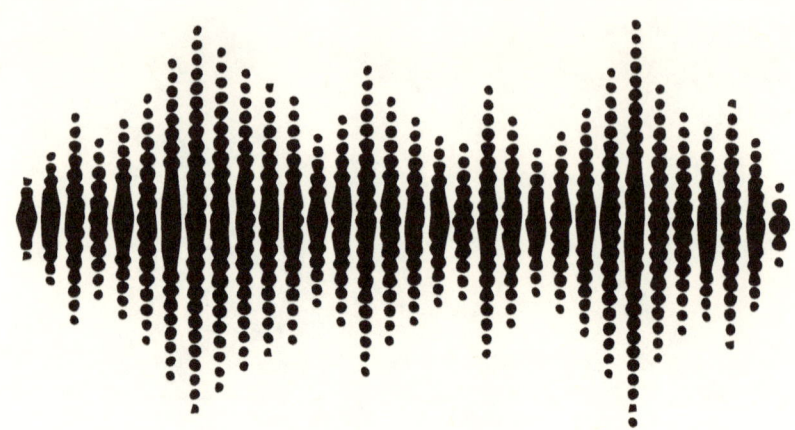

Nineteen
FADING ECHOES

Sometimes, I get flashbacks.
But not just of moments I've lived.
Of places I've never been.
Of feelings that don't belong to this lifetime.
Of something beyond this world —
like a memory from before I arrived here.

It's hard to explain.

It's like I can pull thoughts from the past with such clarity —
like I lived it all just yesterday.
Every joy.
Every scar.
Every goodbye.

And yet...
recently, it's all begun to slip.
The last seven, maybe ten years of my life —
they've started to fade.

Not gone.
Just… muted.
As if the film reel is out of focus.
As if my mind can't hold the weight of all of it anymore.

There are moments I want to remember.
Moments I try to revisit —
not because they were perfect, but because they were mine.
But they don't stay.
The images flicker.
The feelings get tangled.
The timelines blur.

And I don't know why.

Maybe I'm evolving.
Maybe the version of me that lived those memories is no longer who I am now.
Maybe some memories leave us when we've outgrown them —
or when they've already served their purpose.

But it's strange…
because there are times I just want to get lost in a thought.
To sit with it.
Feel it.
Let it breathe life into me again.

And yet the memory doesn't stay.

It visits.
It brushes past.
It disappears.

Almost like it's reminding me —
"You're not meant to stay there anymore."

And maybe that's what this is.
A quiet form of letting go.
Not because I want to — but because I need to.
Because the past no longer defines me.
Because I'm being called to the present now.

Still…

there's a part of me that misses those echoes.
The ones that felt more real than reality sometimes.
The ones that made me feel like I belonged somewhere…
even if it wasn't here.

Twenty
WHAT I WANT TO TELL THE YOUNGER ME

If I could sit beside you right now…
I wouldn't say much at first.
I'd just hold you.
I'd let you rest your head,
because I know how tired you are — even if you never said it out loud.

You've always been the quiet fighter.
The one who smiled through confusion,
laughed through sadness,
stood strong even when the world made you feel small.

And I see you.
I remember every moment you tried to be brave for people who never gave you the space to be vulnerable.
I remember how you looked for love in places that only taught you what it wasn't.

I remember how you questioned if you were too much —
too emotional, too intense, too different.

But you weren't too much.
You were just you.
And that was always more than enough.

I want to tell you…
none of it was your fault.
The way they treated you.
The things they didn't say.
The love they withheld.
The moments you blamed yourself for being "too sensitive" —
they were never reflections of your weakness.
They were proof of your heart.

You didn't need to earn love.
You were love.

And if the world didn't see that,
it was never because you lacked something.
It was because they couldn't recognize what they weren't ready to receive.

I wish you didn't carry so much guilt.
So much silence.
So many "what-ifs."

I wish you knew that the way you cared so deeply wasn't a flaw —
it was your gift.

You didn't grow up in the safest hands.
You weren't always met with soft words.
But you grew anyway.
And somehow… you turned into someone beautiful.
Not perfect.
But real.

So here's what I want to say to you, younger me:

Keep going.

I know you're tired.
I know you don't always understand why things happened the way they did.
But one day, you'll look back and realize —
you were never lost.
You were *becoming*.

You'll learn to forgive.
You'll learn to breathe softer.
You'll stop blaming yourself for not knowing things you were never taught.

And most of all —
you'll learn to love yourself in ways no one ever showed you how.

So don't rush.
Don't harden.
And don't ever let this world make you feel like you're not enough.

Because one day…
you'll be writing this.
And you'll realize —
you always were.

Twenty One
IF THIS IS THE LAST PAGE

If this is the last page I ever write...
then let it be honest.
Let it carry the weight of everything I've felt,
and the softness of everything I've become.

Let it say that I lived — not perfectly,
but fully.
With a heart that cracked open more times than it should have...
and still beat louder than silence.

Let it be known that I loved.
Not just others —
but eventually, *myself*.
Even when it was hard.
Even when it felt undeserved.

Let this page say I survived things I never spoke of.
That I bled in silence, but never let the world see me unravel.

That I smiled when I wanted to disappear.
That I stood when I had every reason to fall.

Let it hold the truth —
that I've been seen through a thousand lenses,
but rarely through the one that actually reflected me.
That I've been admired, misunderstood, even romanticized —
but few stayed long enough to know me.

And still…
I stayed true.
I stayed real.
I never stopped becoming who I was meant to be.

And if this is the last page —
then let it carry my prayer.

That all I've been through wasn't in vain.
That someone out there, maybe even you,
read these words and felt less alone.
Felt seen.
Felt safe.
Felt… understood.

Because that's all I ever wanted.

Not fame.
Not perfection.
Just connection.
Just meaning.

So if this is the last page…
thank you.

For making it this far.
For holding this space with me.

For listening — even when it was heavy.
For seeing me.
And if you carry anything from these words,
let it be this:

I am someone who felt deeply in a world that often tried to stay numb.

Someone who gave without keeping score.
Someone who waited when others rushed.
Someone who never stopped believing there was more to this life than what we see.

And maybe — that was enough.

Maybe this wasn't a story about pain after all.
Maybe it was always a story about light —
the kind you protect, the kind you grow into,
the kind you quietly leave behind for someone else to find.

And maybe, just maybe —
this isn't the last page at all.
Maybe it's just the beginning…
of someone else's healing.

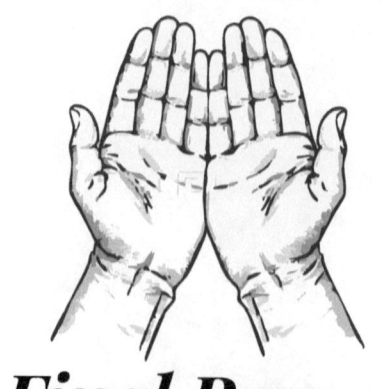

Final Prayer

Dear God,

If these pages meant something,
let them reach the hearts that needed them most.
Let them fall into the hands of someone who was silently breaking…
and remind them that they're still here for a reason.

Thank you for carrying me when I didn't have the strength to walk.
For the nights You stayed, even when I thought I was alone.
For the light You placed inside me — the one I sometimes tried to dim.

I don't know where this road leads from here.
But I trust You.

Not because I see the whole path,
but because I know You see me.

I offer this book — this story — as a prayer in itself.
A testimony of what it means to survive quietly.
To feel deeply.
To lose… and still rise.

If these words planted even the smallest seed of hope in someone —
then it was worth it.
I leave the rest to You.

Amen.

P.S.

No matter what happens, I'll still choose love—because that's who I am. I only know how to love, and as I walk to the very ends of this world, I'll continue giving kindness and light.

Atlas

www.ingramcontent.com/pod-product-compliance
Lightning Source LLC
Chambersburg PA
CBHW021638080526
44584CB00015BA/1530